TRAVEL doodles For Kids

ANITA WOOD
DRAWINGS BY **CHRIS SABATINO**

GIBBS SMITH
TO ENRICH AND INSPIRE HUMANKIND

Manufactured in Salt Lake City, Utah, USA, in
January 2018 by Artistic Printing

First Edition
22 21 20 19 18   10 9 8 7 6

Published by
Gibbs Smith
P.O. Box 667
Layton, Utah 84041

1.800.835.4993 orders
www.gibbs-smith.com

Designed by Melissa Dymock

Gibbs Smith books are printed on either recycled,
100% post-consumer waste, FSC-certified papers or
on paper produced from sustainable PEFC-certified
forest/controlled wood source. Learn more at www.
pefc.org.

ISBN 13: 978-1-4236-2454-7

For my BFF, Cindy.
The journey is always the best part.
Where are we headed to next?
—AW

How many times have you heard or said,
"Are we there yet?" Keep score here.

COUNT BOARD

ARE WE THERE YET?

What did the elephant pack in his trunk?

Hilarious Hometowns

What's making everybody itch
in Scratch Ankle, Alabama?

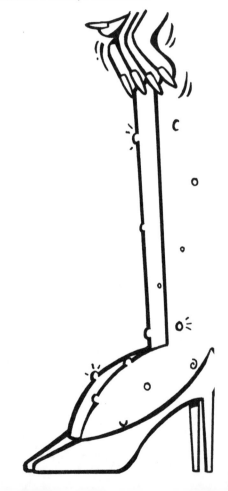

Design a fun tread pattern on this tire.

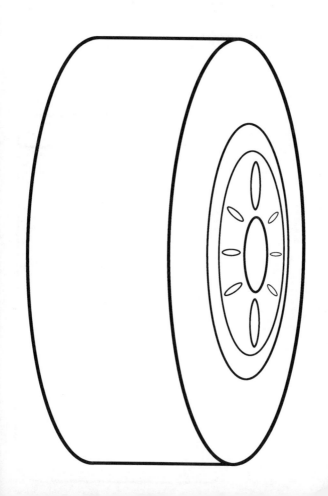

Customize these mud flaps.

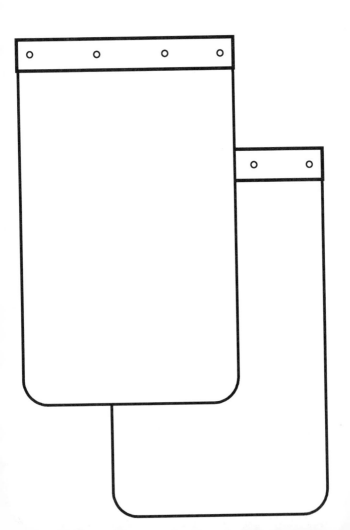

Slug bug! Keep track of all the VW bugs that you spot. What color do you see the most?

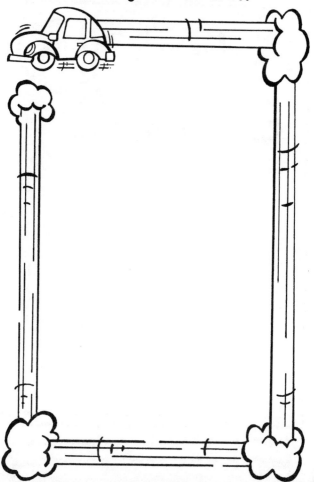

Funny Signs

Fill in the blank.

Draw a bunch of bugs
on the windshield.

Hilarious Hometowns

Eek, Alaska, is being overrun with what?

Doodle some graffiti on the train car.

How many birds can you draw on the telephone wires?

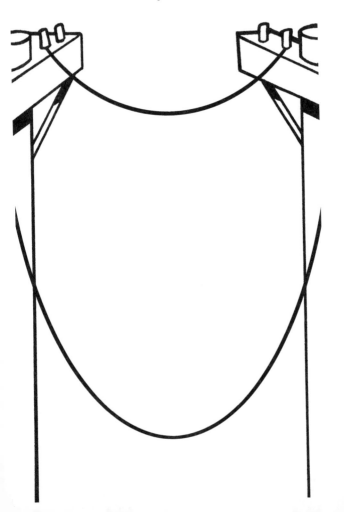

Decorate this window with figures
that depict your family members.

Add a hood ornament on this car.

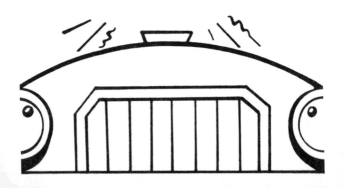

Hilarious Hometowns

What's lurking around the corner in Surprise, Arizona?

What's creeping up from behind?

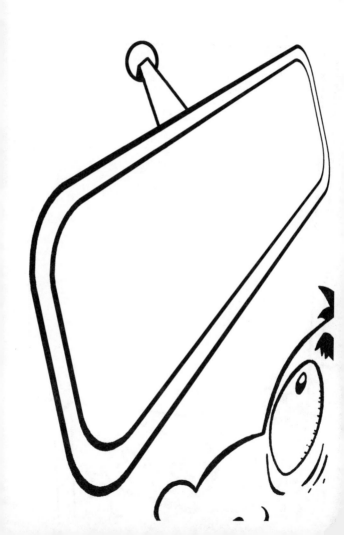

Alligator crossing. Complete the sign.

Fill the night sky with planets and stars.

Draw a bridge across the Grand Canyon.

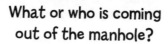
What or who is coming out of the manhole?

Hilarious Hometowns

Something doesn't smell very good
in Stinking Bay, Arkansas. Draw it.

Ninety-nine bottles of _____ on the wall. Add your own spin to this fun car song and draw your favorite beverage.

Weird Roadside Architecture

This building in Chester, West Virginia, looks like a teakettle!

WHAT'S THAT WHISTLING?

Draw a sign on the tanker. What's inside? Soda? Chocolate milk? Slime?

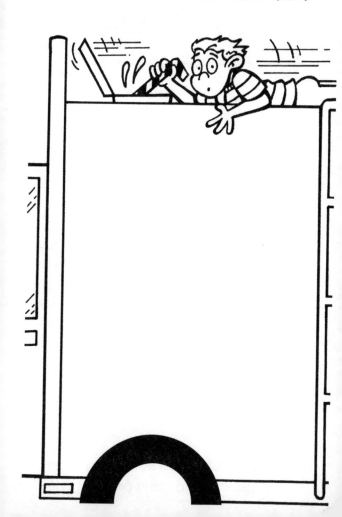

Spell out a message on the
desert sand using rocks.

Hilarious Hometowns

The Grumpy Bunch is loose in Happy Camp, California. Draw the not-so-happy expressions on their faces.

Who (or what) is strapped
into the roller blades?

Draw some crazy designs on these domes at St. Basil's Cathedral in Moscow, Russia.

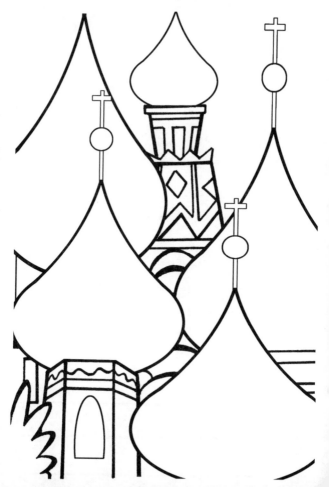

Finish building a fantastic
time-traveling machine.

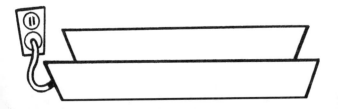

When do you travel to?
Somewhere in the past or future?

TIME LINE

150,000,000 B.C   2000 B.C.   1850 A.D.   5000 A.D.

Create your own traffic jam.

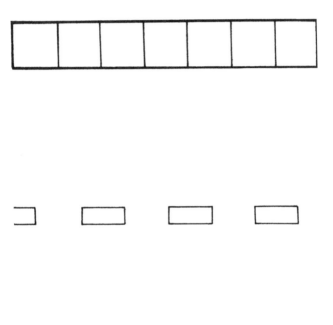

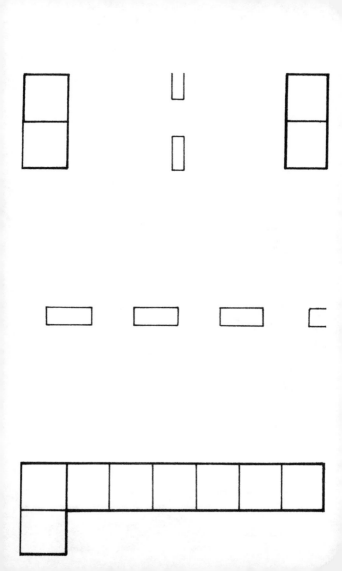

What's being hauled on this flatbed trailer?

Hilarious Hometowns

What's so scary about Spooky Mountain, Colorado?

Fill in the word M_ss_ss_pp_
with some crazy googlie eyes.

What stays in a corner but travels around the world? A postage stamp! Draw some fun stamps from all over the world.

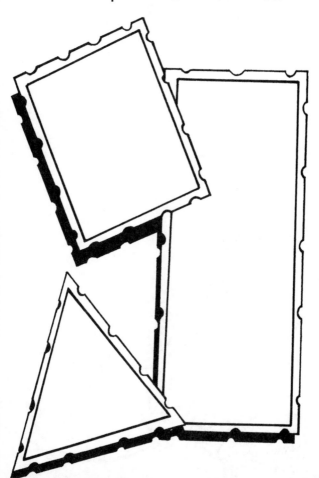

Dino Airways. Add a cabin
of seats on its back.

Weird Roadside Architecture

This house in Grand Marais, Michigan,
is built to look like a pickle barrel.

What's been left on the
side of the road?

Funny Signs

Fill in the blank.

Tic-tac-toe

Hilarious Hometowns

Give the citizens of Whigville,
Connecticut, some fancy hairdos.

What is the little old lady selling
at her roadside stand?

Swimming in a pool in the middle of the ocean. Where are you?

Answer: On a cruise ship.

What's holding up the Leaning Tower of Pisa?

You're participating in the Gatineau Hot Air Balloon Festival in Québec, Canada. Finish drawing your balloon.

What do these bumper stickers say?

Hilarious Hometowns

What is hatching in
Owls Nest, Delaware?

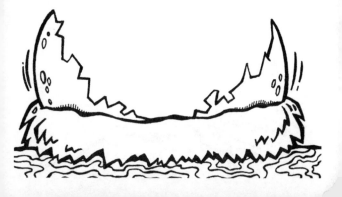

Yellowstone National Park's famous
Old Faithful geyser just erupted.
What came shooting out?

Funny Signs

Fill in the blank.

Draw a map that leads from your house to your vacation destination.

How many cows can you count?
Write "Moo" for each one you see.

Hilarious Hometowns

Give this bucking horse in
Yeehaw Junction, Florida, a rider.

Cover the suitcase with stickers from different states or countries.

Who (or what) is pulling the rickshaw?

Send a postcard to a friend.

What did one boulder say to the other in Talking Rock, Georgia?

There's a sea monster
attacking the cruise ship!

Hilarious Hometowns

It's Father's Day in Papa, Hawaii,
and you gave your dad a
crazy necktie. Draw it.

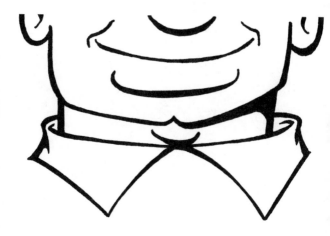

Haunted beach.
Draw a sand-witch.

How many different kinds of
seashells can you find at the
beach? Fill the fishing net.

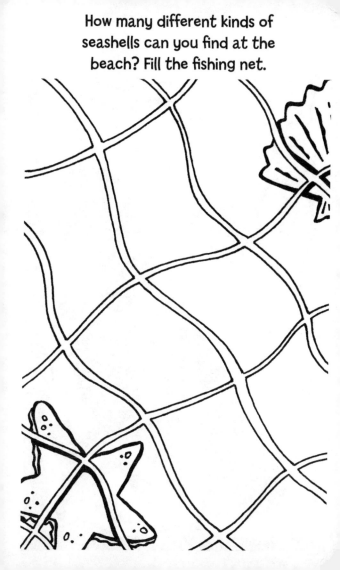

Help the chicken cross the road.

Hilarious Hometowns

What's growing on
Hairy Hill, Alberta, Canada?

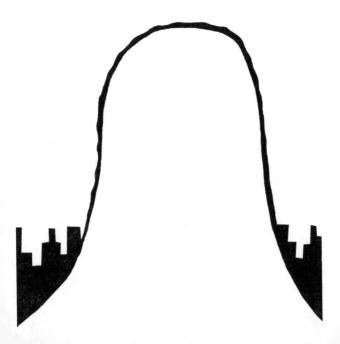

Weird Roadside Architecture

This house in Signal Mountain,
Tennessee, was built to look like a UFO.

I DON'T REMEMBER PARKING HERE!

What do you think the Florida
Keys really look like?

If you went on a journey to the Earth's center, what would you expect to find?

Hilarious Hometowns

What's rattling around
Skeleton Creek, Idaho?

Elephant trekking! Draw a fancy carrier on the elephant's back.

What are these dogs
pulling behind them?

Arrrrrgh! You've stowed away on a pirate ship. What be her name and what does she look like, matey?

Seeing the pyramids by camel.
Does the camel have one hump or two?

Funny Signs

Fill in the blank.

Traveling along the Extraterrestrial
Highway in Nevada you spot an alien
and its UFO. What do they look like?

Hilarious Hometowns

What's making these people blush in Embarrass, Illinois?

How can you turn a dog into a cat?
Turn the first word into the second
word by changing one letter at a time,

Example: dog   dot

             pig

             hot

             hand

             hate

             cow

             sick

making sure all the words in between
are real words too! (It may take
more than four words to do it.)

cot

cat

sty

tub

foot

love

hen

well

Baby it's *hot* outside!
Draw the world's largest
thermometer in Baker, California.

Weird Roadside Architecture

This building in Newark, Ohio,
looks like a picnic basket.

Collect-a-Critter. Draw some creepy bugs you've found while camping near Spider Creek, British Columbia, Canada.

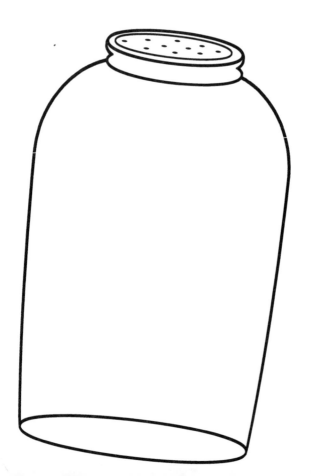

Hilarious Hometowns

Who's winning the race in
Toad Hop, Indiana?

I spy with my little eye. Mark off each of the things below when you see one.

Fill the cooler with all your favorite snacks.

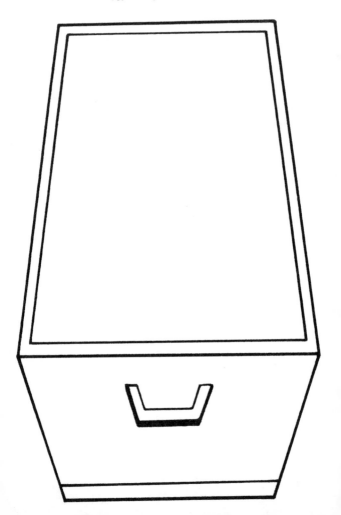

Hilarious Hometowns

Rabbits have overrun Carrot
Creek, Alberta, Canada.

Draw some steam rising and lava flowing out of Mauna Loa Volcano in Hawaii.

The Dot Game

Take turns drawing lines from one dot to another; when you create a square or triangle, fill it in with your initials. The one with the most squares or triangles wins. Play with your brother, sister, or friend.

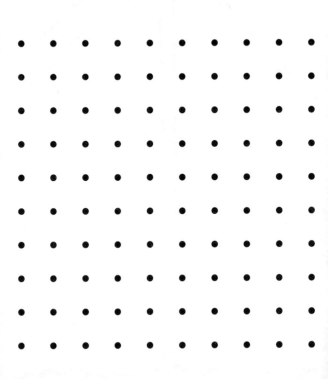

Your camping tent is a lot bigger than it seems. What's inside?

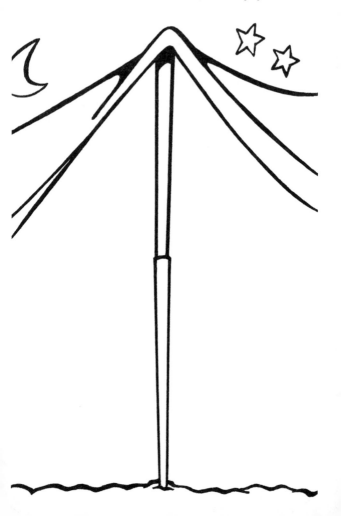

Hilarious Hometowns

Everything's on a slant
in Diagonal, Iowa.

Fall in New England. Color these leaves and add some of your own.

Welcome to Mammoth Cave in Kentucky. Add some stalactites (descending from the ceiling) and stalagmites (rising from the floor).

You're on a dinosaur dig in Dinosaur Provincial Park, Alberta, Canada. What have you uncovered?

Draw some ancient markings
on these rock walls.

Hilarious Hometowns

Yes, there is something
disgusting in Gross, Kansas.

Draw some of the bears and other
animals that might be found
in the Great Bear Rainforest in
British Columbia, Canada.

Car Bingo

How many of these signs can you spot?

REST AREA

FREE

DETOUR

TRUCK ROUTE

ONE WAY

Draw the cool fish you find while scuba diving in the Caribbean.

Hilarious Hometowns

Who is squealing "wee, wee, wee" all
the way home to Pig, Kentucky.

Next stop Mars!
Draw your spaceship.

It's 1854, and your family is
heading west to California. Finish
drawing your covered wagon.

How many different state license plates can you spot? Fill in a plate with each state name.

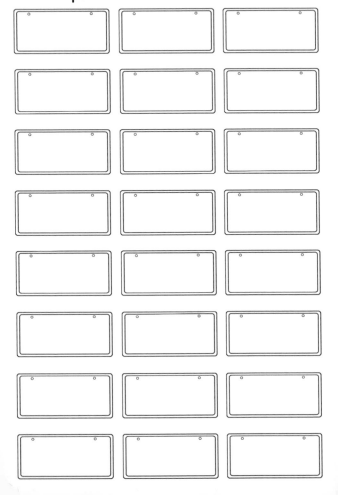

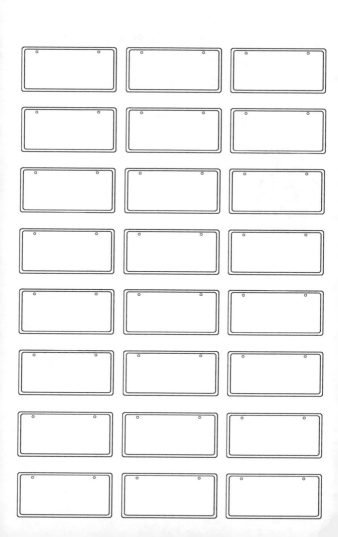

Weird Roadside Architecture

Cadillac Ranch in Amarillo, Texas, features a row of brightly painted old Cadillacs half-buried in the ground. Draw some more!

Hilarious Hometowns

What's making these people sleepy in Yawn, Louisiana?

Heading for the Florida Everglades!
Draw the houseboat you'll
be staying on.

Lions and tigers, oh my!
What else have you seen
while on safari?

Finish drawing the airplane that will take you on a great adventure.

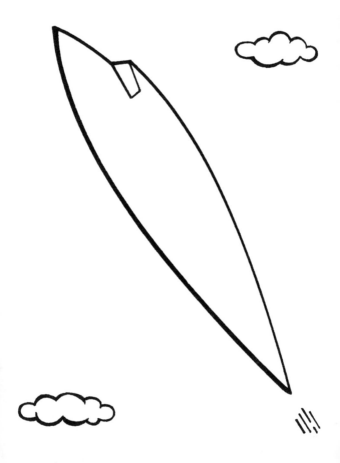

Mom and Dad went on vacation
and all they brought me was
this stupid _____.

Draw the rest of the
Golden Gate Bridge.

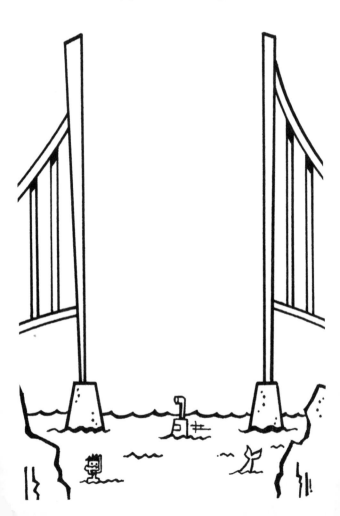

Hilarious Hometowns

What are they growing in
Bald Head, Maine?

What does the personalized license plate on this convertible say?

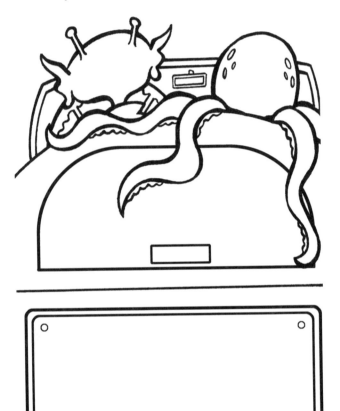

Draw the friendly spirits that hang
out in this western ghost town.

Add some more headstones with funny names in Boot Hill Cemetery in Tombstone, Arizona.

Hangman

A great game to play with your brother or sister. Decide which of you will think of a word and which of you will guess the letters. Try not to hang the poor fellow!

Hilarious Hometowns

It's raining coins in
Catchpenny, Maryland.

How many different trucking
companies can you spot? Make
a list or draw their logos.

Troll bridge up ahead. Draw the troll that's collecting tolls.

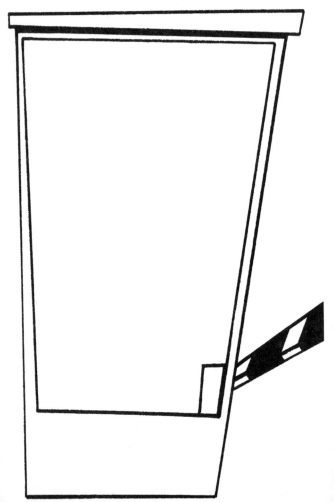

Draw the troll bridge too!

Weird Roadside Architecture

This house in Hellam, Pennsylvania,
looks like a shoe.

Hilarious Hometowns

Draw a bird from Buzzards
Bay, Massachusetts.

Draw the big gorilla who's swatting at planes atop the Empire State Building.

Complete this section of the Great Wall of China.

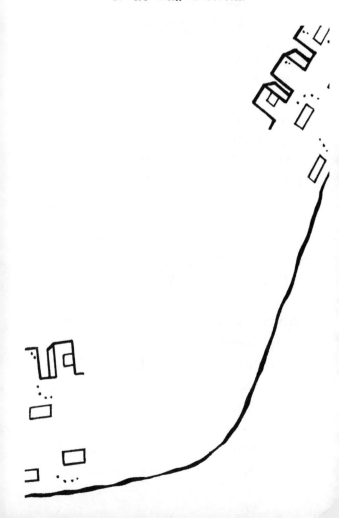

World Word Search

Let's see if you can find
the following words.

```
X  U  H  C  C  I  P  U  H  C  A  M
L  Q  W  H  I  T  E  H  O  U  S  E
A  T  Y  L  A  T  I  S  F  Y  P  G
N  A  Q  L  R  G  F  L  S  H  H  N
A  J  I  O  H  K  F  W  X  Q  I  E
C  M  L  N  K  R  E  M  L  I  N  H
A  A  H  D  J  O  L  N  L  P  X  E
M  H  C  O  M  X  T  A  I  G  J  N
A  A  I  N  B  U  O  D  R  A  V  O
N  L  N  C  Z  L  W  Q  Z  T  P  T
A  K  U  U  R  S  E  M  O  R  E  S
P  E  M  A  D  E  R  T  O  N  V  P
```

White House	Notre Dame
Eiffel Tower	Taj Mahal
Stonehenge	Panama Canal
Luxor	Machu Picchu
Kremlin	Rome
Sphinx	Spain
London	Italy
Petra	Munich

Weird Roadside Architecture

Draw the world's largest piggy bank
in Coleman, Alberta, Canada.

Draw some sails on this sailboat.

You're going to a dude ranch, so you'll need a pair of chaps, boots, and a cowboy hat. Draw them here.

Hilarious Hometowns

Who's flying over Witch Lake, Michigan?

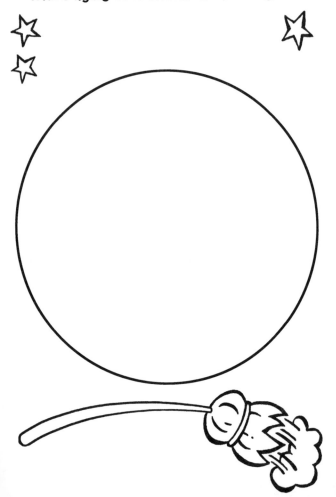

Radio Bingo

I heard it on the radio. . . . Listen for the following words and mark them off when you hear them.

song	contest	website	concert
phone	**FREE**	register	sunny
tickets	home	accident	business
time	traffic	news	score

You've been panning for gold in
Barkerville, British Columbia, Canada.
Draw the biggest nugget you found.

Something is attacking the Eiffel Tower!

Where would you go on your dream vacation?

Weird Roadside Architecture

This ice cream shop in Rockingham, North Carolina, looks like a gigantic strawberry.

THAT BERRY NEEDS TO DIET!

UMM HMM.

What kind of top secret weapon is being transported in this truck?

Hilarious Hometowns

What's lurking around
Castle Danger, Minnesota?

Slower traffic, keep right.
What's causing the traffic jam?

Give these plain old construction cones a makeover.

Speeding down the autobahn in Europe. How fast are you going?

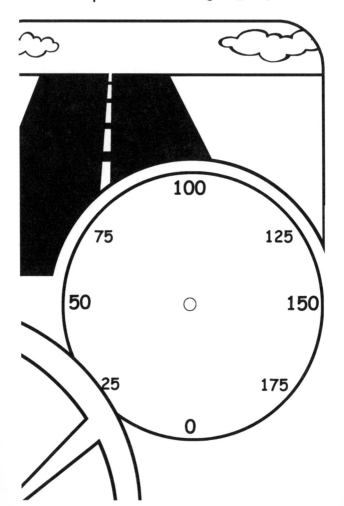

At the aquarium. What kind of sea animals are in the petting pool?

How many three-letter words
can you spell from the letters
on passing license plates?

Example: PSA = Sap

Hilarious Hometowns

What's sizzling in Bacon, Mississippi?

Scan the sky for some unusual cloud formations and draw what you see.

Hilarious Hometowns

What will you find in Old Man's Pocket, Ontario, Canada.

Goblin Valley State Park in Utah is
full of all kinds of spooky and weird
rock formations. Draw a few.

Fill this tide pool with colorful anemones, spiky sea urchins, crabs, and sea stars.

Decorate this old bus before
heading out on a road trip.

Riding the cable cars in San Francisco.
Draw a cable car.

Hilarious Hometowns

What's being created in this spooky
laboratory in Frankenstein, Missouri?

Whale of a tale! While fishing in Jellybean Lake, Ontario, Canada, you hook a new species of fish.

Where are you? (Hints: It's often referred to as "The Happiest Place on Earth" and is home to a famous mouse.) Draw some characters you might see there.

Hilarious Hometowns

Who's leaving footprints
in Muddy, Montana?

Viva Las Vegas! What world-famous landmarks can you find here in a smaller size? (Ask Mom and Dad if you need help.)

What is on the back side of Mt. Rushmore?

Funny Signs

Fill in the blank.

Student Driver. Give this car
some training wheels.

Hilarious Hometowns

Who's your Valentine in Valentine, Nebraska? Finish the Valentine's card.

Who or what's riding on the motorcycle?

Running the rapids down the wild
Snake River in the Yukon Territory,
Canada. Draw your raft.

Where are you? Standing in a crown
in the middle of New York Harbor,
over 200 feet above the ground.

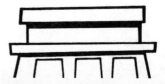

Hilarious Hometowns

The action figures and windup
characters have come to
life in Toy, Nevada.

Where will this ticket take you?

Silly Story

Take turns adding a sentence.

There once was an elephant named Skippy.

_____

_____

_____

_____

_____

_____

_____

_____

_____

_____

What is hurtling over Niagara Falls?

Hilarious Hometowns

What's for lunch in Sandwich,
New Hampshire?

What am I? I have a large crack
in me and I used to hang in
Independence Hall in Philadelphia.

Answer: Liberty Bell.

What is hanging from St. Louis's Gateway Arch?

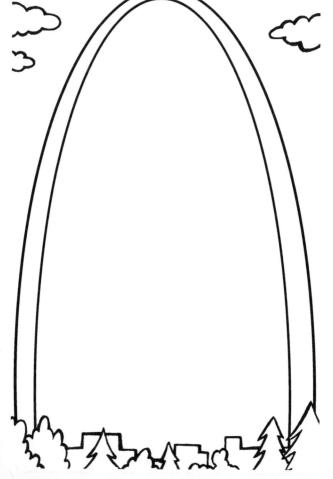

All Mixed Up. Unscramble the names of these cities.

Atlanta
Buffalo
Calgary
Chicago
Denver
Ontario
Philadelphia
Phoenix
Sacramento

1. agcohic _____

2. dpelhipalhia _____

3. artonio _____

4. ramcentosa _____

5. talatna _____

6. agrycla _____

7. afobulf _____

8. nrevde _____

9. nioxeph _____

Where are you? You've got one foot in New Mexico, one hand in Colorado, one hand in Arizona, and one foot in Utah. Draw the rest of the state outlines.

Answer: Four Corners Monument.

Draw the world's coolest waterslide.

Hilarious Hometowns

Who's wearing these funny pants
in Buttzville, New Jersey.

What's green, has four legs, and two trunks? Two seasick tourists with their luggage! Finish the drawing.

A giant sponge soaked up all the water in this lake. Draw the giant sponge and everything lying on the bottom of the lake.

WELL, THERE GOES THE NEIGHBORHOOD.

Suzie, the world's largest softball is six feet in diameter! You can see her in Chauvin, Alberta, Canada. Give her a happy face.

Hilarious Hometowns

What's for dessert in Pie
Town, New Mexico?

Roadside Alphabet

Try to spot something that begins
with each letter of the alphabet.
Write the word after each letter.

A _____

B _____

C _____

D _____

E _____

F _____

G _____

H _____

I _____

J _____

K _____

L _____

M _____

N _____

O _____

P _____

Q _____

R _____

S _____

T _____

U _____

V _____

W _____

X _____

y _____

Z _____

This revolving door leads to a strange world. What's coming out of it?

Prairie dog holes.
What's popping out?

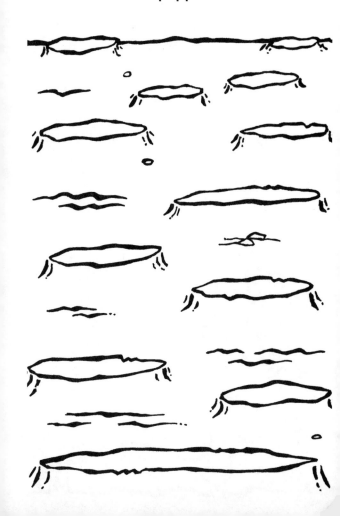

This snail misses its house.
Give it one.

Ladies and gentlemen! Presenting
the "man-eating chicken."
What does it look like?

Hilarious Hometowns

It's Doodle Day in Doodletown, New York.
Fill the page with your favorite doodles.

Where was the Declaration of Independence signed? Add your signature, and have some of your friends add theirs.

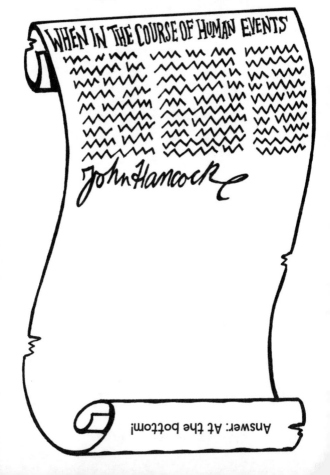

WHEN IN THE COURSE OF HUMAN EVENTS

John Hancock

Answer: At the bottom!

What lies at the bottom of the sea and shivers?

Answer: A nervous wreck.

New York is also called the "Big Apple." Draw a juicy apple here.

How do bees get to school? Draw it.

Answer: By school buzz!

Hilarious Hometowns

Pick something to draw in
Boogertown, North Carolina.

Scavenger hunt.
Try to spot the following.

What do you see through the spyglass?

What kind of dinosaurs are roaming through the park?

Hilarious Hometowns

What's so electrifying in
Zap, North Dakota?

You look out the window of the plane—
and something is staring back at you!

The stagecoach is being robbed
by outlaws! Finish drawing it.

Road Trip Tunes. How many songs can you think of that mention driving, cars, cities, and trips? Ask Mom and Dad to help. (Examples: "Running on Empty," "Life Is a Highway," "On the Road Again")

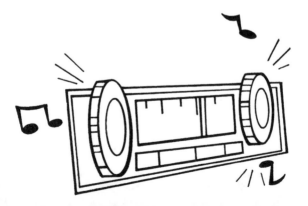

Hoover Dam, on the border of
Arizona and Nevada, is holding
back what instead of water?

HOOVER DAM

Hilarious Hometowns

Even the trees are edible
in Candy Town, Ohio.

A bird has nested inside
this giant cactus.

There's a silly monster that lives in Crater Lake National Park in Oregon. What does it look like?

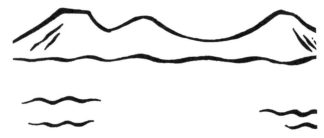

You've been made Junior Park Ranger.
Finish drawing your badge.

Hilarious Hometowns

The streets are being flooded with
milk in Cookietown, Oklahoma. Doodle
and dunk your favorite cookies.

Fill in the face of the compass.

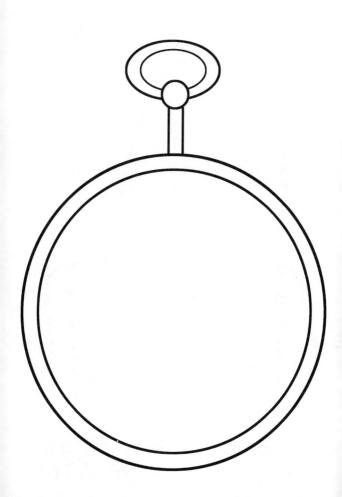

Idaho is famous for potatoes.
Give this one a face, arms, and feet.

You've been stranded on a deserted island. Build a hut using the wreckage from your boat.

Dot-to-Dot

See if you can join all the dots
with eight straight lines. You must
not lift your pencil from the paper
and you can't cross the same dot
more than once. Good luck!

Cliff dwellings. Draw some ancient stone ruins.

Hilarious Hometowns

What's going down in Drain, Oregon?

Armchair Traveler. Add a huge bunch of helium balloons to this easy chair and get ready for adventure.

Instead of a paddle wheel, this riverboat is powered by what?

The Space Needle in Seattle, Washington, is about to be threaded by a giant what?

Hilarious Hometowns

Things are a little strange in Normalville, Pennsylvania. What weird things would you see? An upside-down house? A cow in a tree? A dog on roller skates?

At 60 feet tall, the world's largest rocking horse resides in Gumeracha, South Australia. Draw it.

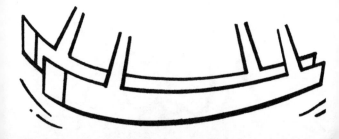

You've just spotted the ever-elusive jackalope. Give this jackrabbit some antlers.

On tour! Your favorite singer/band just drove by. Decorate the side of their bus.

Funny Signs

Fill in the blank.

Hilarious Hometowns

You're on your way to a motorcycle gathering at Hog Island, Rhode Island. Finish drawing your hog.

Where is this hitchhiker headed?

Roller Coaster. Are these kids having some crazy fun or are they just plain scared? Finish their faces.

Hilarious Hometowns

What's keeping everybody up in
Wide Awake, South Carolina.

Give this banana-juggling
monkey a unicycle to ride.

Have fun collecting memorabilia from your trips, such as tickets to shows, parks, rides, and museums, and keep them here.

Hilarious Hometowns

Why is everybody laughing in Saint-Louis-du-Ha! Ha!, Quebec, Canada.

Decorate the circus train cars.

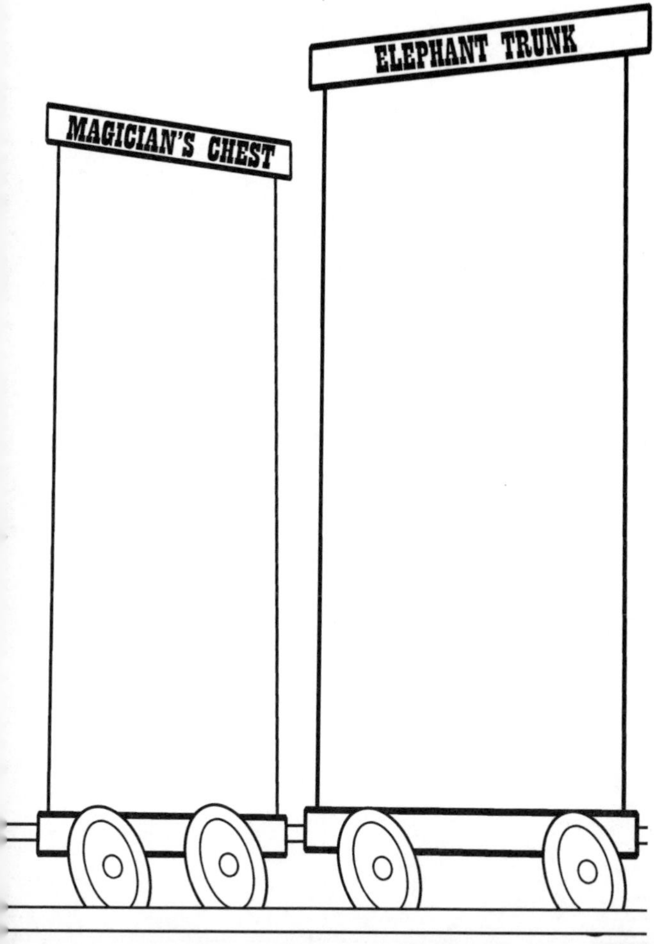

MAGICIAN'S CHEST

ELEPHANT TRUNK

How many different car company logos can you spot? There are lots of 'em! Draw each one you see.

Hilarious Hometowns

Finish drawing the winning
pageant contestant in
Prairie Queen, South Dakota.

While diving for pearls you find a gigantic oyster shell, and what you discover inside is not a pearl!

Silly Sentences

Make up a short, funny phrase or sentence
using the letters on passing license
plates as the first letter of each word.

Examples: LHD = Little Hairy Dog
LEP = Let's Eat Pizza

You've just wandered into a village of headhunters in the Amazon. Before hightailing it out of there, draw their collection of shrunken heads.

STAY FOR DINNER?

If you were a car, truck, boat, motorcycle, or airplane, what would you look like? Choose one and draw it.

Hilarious Hometowns

What's your favorite thing to
eat in Yum Yum, Tennessee?

You are a fierce gladiator in ancient Rome getting ready for a chariot race. Trick out your ride.

Sailing to Skull Island on a mysterious adventure! What gigantic creature is waiting for you on the beach?

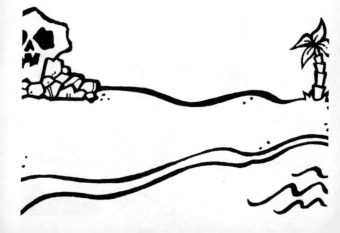

Draw a fancy saddlebag
for your horse.

It's not a mirage. You've stumbled
upon a desert oasis. Draw it.

Hilarious Hometowns

What's for breakfast in
Oatmeal, Texas?

That's an awfully big chicken!
Draw a saddle on this ostrich.

Draw the itty-bitty dog that's sniffing this fire hydrant!

Marooned on an alien planet.
Draw some of your new BFFs.

Who is that traveler?
Pick out a passing car or truck and
make up a story about who they
are and where they're going.

Wow! Those sure aren't regular
water skis she has on!

Car Bingo

How many of these things can you spot?

Hilarious Hometowns

Who's coming down Devil's Slide, Utah?

Instead of wheels, give this airplane
some other kind of landing gear.

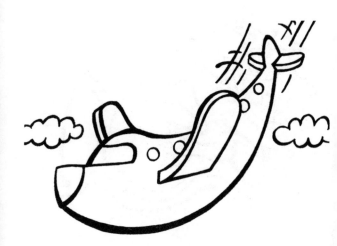

Let's give this turtle a faster
way to get around.

How many cars and trucks can you spot that are named after animals? Keep track here.

Rabbit

Ram

Hilarious Hometowns

What's bugging you in
Mosquitoville, Vermont.

Give this centipede some jogging shoes.

This vehicle is shaped like
a giant hot dog!

Hilarious Hometowns

What's invading Roaches Corner, Virginia?

Turn these shapes into a plane, train, boat, and car.

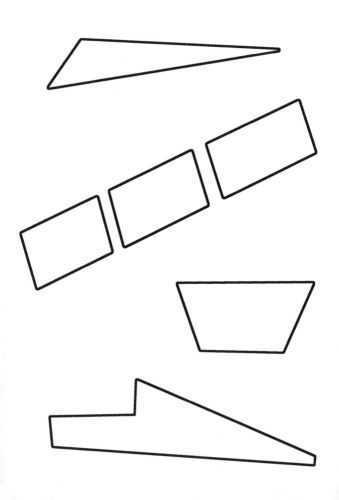

How does this helicopter fly?

X marks the spot!
Complete this treasure map.

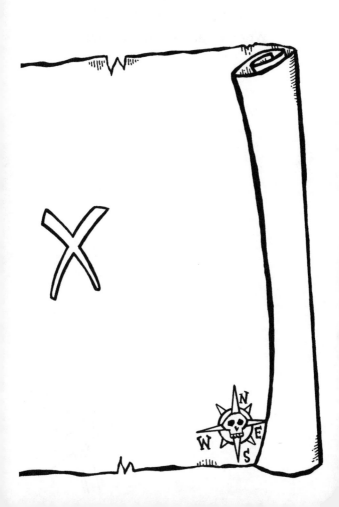

Hilarious Hometowns

No parents allowed in
Kid Valley, Washington!
What would you do all day?

What kind of slithery critters are in this swamp?

Hilarious Hometowns

What's growing on the trees in
Crab Orchard, West Virginia?

This dog is enjoying a ride. Draw the car or truck he's hanging out of.

Hilarious Hometowns

This poor fellow needs a friend
in Imalone, Wisconsin.

How fast should you go?
Fill in the speed limit sign.

A skunk has taken up residence in the
port-a-potty! Pew! Finish drawing it.

Locked alone in the museum
at night, and some of the
exhibits have come to life!

Funny Signs

Fill in the blank.

What will you find at the
end of this road in Chocolate
Mountain, Alberta, Canada?

Collect Them All!

Available at bookstores or
directly from Gibbs Smith

1.800.835.4993

www.pocketdoodles.com